Sun and The Shadows
100 Poems of nature and beauty

Omar H Malik

Grosvenor House
Publishing Limited

All rights reserved
Copyright © Omar H Malik, 2025

The right of Omar H Malik to be identified as the author of this work has been asserted in accordance with Section 78 of the Copyright, Designs and Patents Act 1988

The book cover is copyright to Omar H Malik

This book is published by
Grosvenor House Publishing Ltd
Link House
140 The Broadway, Tolworth, Surrey, KT6 7HT.
www.grosvenorhousepublishing.co.uk

This book is sold subject to the conditions that it shall not, by way of trade or otherwise, be lent, resold, hired out or otherwise circulated without the author's or publisher's prior consent in any form of binding or cover other than that in which it is published and without a similar condition including this condition being imposed on the subsequent purchaser.

A CIP record for this book
is available from the British Library

Paperback ISBN 978-1-83615-265-1

I dedicate this book to my granddaughter

Jessica Bettridge

celebrating her coming of age

CONTENTS

SUN AND THE SHADOWS	1
BEAUTY	3
BEAUTY AND THE BLIND	7
SUNRISE SUNSET	8
A LEAF'S LEASE OF LIFE	11
A MOMENT TO CHERISH	12
ATUMN LEAVES	13
AUTUMN	14
AZALEA	16
BABBLING BROOK	17
BIRD IN A CAGE	18
BIRDSONG	20
BLACKBIRD	21
BLOOMING	23
BLUEBELLS	24
BUDDLEIA AND THE BUTTERFLY	25
BUSY BEES	26
BUTTERCUPS	28
CAMELLIA	29
CHERRY BLOSSOMS	30
CHILL WIND'S MONOTONE	31
COLOURS	32
CONKERS	36

COW-PARSLEY	37
COWSLIPS	38
DAFFODIL	39
DAISY	40
DANDELIONS	41
DARK CLOUD	42
DIVINE BRUSH-STROKES	44
DOLPHINS	45
DURDLE DOOR	46
ELEPHANT	47
ETERNALLY SEALED	48
FINGAL'S CAVE	49
FLOWER SONG	50
FORSYTHIA	51
FOUR SEASONS	52
FOXGLOVE	53
FUCHSIA	54
GAZELLE	55
HAWTHORN	57
HONEYSUKLE	58
IN A ROSE GARDEN	59
JASMINE	61
LABURNUM	62
LAVENDER	63
LET THE GARDEN BE MY SHRINE	64
LIGHT AND REFLECTIONS	67
LILY OF THE VALLEY	68

LILY	69
LONE BENCH IN THE PARK	70
MAGNOLIA	72
MARIGOLD	73
MEADOW FLOWERS	74
MIGRATION	75
MOONBEAM	76
MOONLIGHT	77
MOUNTAIN	78
MUSIC IN THE LANDSCAPE	81
NOCTURNE	84
OCEAN WAVES	85
ORCHID	88
PEBBLES	89
PEONY	91
PERIWINKLE	92
RAINBOW	93
RAINDROPS	95
RED POPPY	96
RHODODENDRON	97
RIVER SONG	98
ROBIN REDBREAST	99
ROCKS	100
ROSE	102
SACRED SHRINE	103
SHADOW'S VEIL	105
SNOWDROPS	106

SNOWFLAKES	107
SPIDER'S WEB	108
SPRING'S IN THE AIR	109
SPRINGTIME	111
SQUIRREL	112
STAR LIGHT	113
SUMMER	115
SUN SEA AND SAND	116
SUN SEASONS AND SENTIMENT	117
SUN WIND AND RAIN	118
SWEET DREAMS	119
SWEET PRIMROSE	120
THE CLOUD	121
THE SWAN	123
TRANQUILLITY	124
VOLCANO	126
WATER LILY	128
WATERFALL	129
WILD FLOWERS BY THE WOODLAND WALKS	130
WILD FLOWERS	131
WILD RHODODENDRON	132
WINTER	133
WISTERIA	135

SUN AND THE SHADOWS

Sun's blissful light soft or bright
And shadow's fleeting height
Moving measure for measure
In depiction of pain and pleasure.

Co-habiting in close relation
In a dual core of abstraction,
Co-relation in their composite,
In simplistic semblance opposite.

Light's spreading as sun's rising
And shadow's heads counterpoising,
Two opposites in contradiction
Joined in close contraposition.

Sun's energy and light's potent power,
Then, sunlight and shadows embower,
Another dimension seen in between
When floating clouds tend to join in.

Then, the sun, clouds and the shadows
Flying over hills, forests and meadows
Together a life-line of this living earth
Overseeing mortal's misery and mirth.

Sun and the shadows conveying
Opposite's distinctive displaying
Between light's lively colour spectrums
And shadow's monochrome in doldrums.

Frolicsome at daybreak they start
Then at day's end resting wide apart
Destined forever truly befriended,
Joint endeavor never to be ended.

Sun shining and the shadows blending
Then on a cheery path both wending.
Sun's propensity of intense power
In shadow's harness tends to lower.

Observing sun's dedicated daily flight
And defined lines of day and night,
Then sun and the shadows set aligned
Gave a sense of time in human mind.

In sun's golden chariot's rousing rhyme
Mankind defined the rhythm of time,
Capturing this priceless abstract treasure
In twenty-four hours of clock's measure.

At parting time both seen caressing
In pulchritude and warm embracing.
Two in that spirit of love blending
Witnessing earthly conflicts never ending.

2024

BEAUTY

A discerning mind luminously raised
Awakening in applause aesthetically praised
As beauty is breathing in sublime forms,
A sensory bliss in Divine decorum conforms.

Aesthetics of bare truth and purity,
Natural harmony and human creativity
In sight, sound, taste, touch and fragrance
And in warm embrace of love and romance.

Contoured shapes and forms, light and shade,
Spectrum of colours, sounds musically made,
Complementing and concurring in embrace,
Animating passive passion into emotional grace.

In eloquence of poetry and rhetoric,
In creative minds and hands artistic,
In purity of uncontaminated simplicity,
Seeing beauty in truth as truth is in beauty.

Landscapes and floating skyscapes,
Wildlife of many forms and shapes
And that rejuvenating seasonal wonder!
Beauty in the eyes of the beholder.

Sounds of songbirds sweetly serenading,
Loved one's laughter and intimate bonding,
Transcending spirituality in melodic sound,
Beauty in sound as sounds spellbound.

Taste buds tempted at gourmet invitation
Enjoying a mouth-watering meal sensation,
Thrills and feels of lover's very first kiss,
Beauty in tastes as purity of taste promise.

A mother hugging her child lovingly,
Passionate lovers embracing tenderly,
Hearts touched by compassion and kindness,
Touch of beauty in acts of tenderness.

In an enchanted garden of pure fragrance
Sweet smelling flowers in passionate dance,
Perfumed rose and her added beauty
A smell sensation in perfume's purity.

Innocence of felicity in rhythms of gaiety,
Silence of solitude and peace in tranquillity,
Youth's abundance of expected fertility
And abstract beauty in moral integrity.

Leaving a domain of pain to a realm of pleasure
Enjoying new lease of life in beauty's measure.
Some seeking beauty in opulence and prosperity
And others at home embracing purity of austerity.

Colour and contour in light and shade
As weather patterns form then fade,
Knowledge and its inexhaustible capacity
Exploring delights of life defining beauty.

Beauty breathing in sensorial sensitivity
In perimeters of conceptual duality,
Fertility of life against futility of lifeless
And in latitudes of light and darkness.

Universal appeal of sensual to phenomenal,
May be an object of desire to an individual,
But, beyond physical passion and consumption,
A spiritual connotation, a subject of contemplation.

A phenomenon in abstract measure
Of sensational delight or passive pleasure
In form, spirit, passion and emotion,
In mind, in dream or in imagination.

To witness, fathom and feel the experience
Of soundless voice of solitude as in silence,
Or, in a face of grace and charm may enrapture
As in harmony, order and serenity of nature.

Indication of purposiveness without purpose,
Divine essence and mindfulness in focus,
A purposeful nature in an inspiring orderliness
In clear intimation of our worth but wordless.

Beauty denying the lexicon a clear definition
As ambiguity, duality and relativity in distortion,
In the eyes of the beholder, euphony of sound
And in touch, taste and smell beauty profound.

Between exultation and sacred contemplation
Beauty's breath in wavering incantation,
Beauty in prime sings sweetly and sublime
Only in fleeting time's temporal rhyme.

From 'This Mortal Chime'
From 2016

BEAUTY AND THE BLIND

'Beauty in the eyes
   of the beholder,'
Spare a thought for
   those blind eyes.

That vision's dark spirit
   fighting bolder
Soldiering on
   for that beauty's prize.

Forfeiting senses delight
   forlorn in cruelty,
Yet, promised to those
   eyes of clear vision.

Fates fiendish ferocity
   in that burden of brutality,
Almighty's firm resolve
   and mortal's submission.

2024

SUNRISE SUNSET

The fiery sphere's mystic dance
all-encompassing,
taken for granted and venerating
life goes on,
in struggle and strife, prospects
or hopes torn
days in, days out, this living earth
the sun blessing.

The morning sun smiling
ushering a promising day,
whispering of hope and
possibilities in a new light
slowly energising and negotiating
becoming bright,
waking the sleepy earth
with touch of pure golden ray.

Seeing a day's work over
setting in the far horizon west
and sinking in profusion of colour
under a luminous sky,
colour and beauty inspiring
artists' and poets' imaginative eye,
with promise of another day
finally, setting down to rest.

Beyond comprehension
a faraway gigantic fire ball
generations of mankind awe-inspired
but, clueless,
figured thus far, absence would
render the earth lifeless;
creator as yet unknown,
some believe by a Divine call.

A pure and potent, life generating
and life supporting ray,
by a super-natural order,
life on earth sun had impacted
and over millennia by evolution
lives slowly enacted;
energising or pulverising
sun's presence promised each day.

From millions of miles away
light on its travel path
on a finely balanced course
destined to render,
a fractional deviation will freeze
or burn to cinder,
thus far, helped sustaining
all living beings on earth.

Earth's daily journey through
darkness and sun-light
a defining factor for life,
in time, space and reasons
in moments, hours, days,
weeks, months and seasons
clocking in human minds
twenty-four hours of day and night.

Sun's energy and light
and sea's tireless creative might
in a continuing process
of earth's weather formation
sowing seeds of life but,
not unlocking mysteries of creation;
conjuring weather patterns,
giving living earth's birth-right.

In human consciousness
a trajectory of time-line
on a timeless journey
towards an endless goal
only a fractional image
of the infinite whole,
a dot on eternity's shore,
living earth's lifeline.

2021

A LEAF'S LEASE OF LIFE

In Spring, embellished in bloom seen,
In Summer, wore bright breezy green,
In Autumn, a divinely painted hue,
Final parting hour ruefully in view;
After howling wind's tease and torment
Trying hard to hang on to the last moment.

Following release, a last dance,
Singing the finale in a trance,
Rustling through the whirling wind,
Finally, buried in a heap of own kind.
In Winter, evergreens stay firm and defy
Frost, snow and chill wind's howling cry.

From 'Reflections'
20. 11. 2014

A MOMENT TO CHERISH

A star-spangled warm summer's night,
Full moon, not a hint of cloud in sight,
My heart feels happy and content,
Let this be a rare motionless moment!

My love of life close beside me,
The most beautiful sight I live to see,
Stars twinkling in the night sky,
I see reflection in her sparkling eye.

A moment to treasure and cherish,
Time dared not attempt to perish!
Oh no, this visual sensory and vivid imagery
I will treasure in my inner core of memory.

Moments, time doesn't allow us to borrow,
Moments of happiness or moments of sorrow,
One solitary entrance, then the final exit,
Time never meant to turn back and revisit.

An eternal journey through wondrous hollow,
Footsteps only memories cherish and follow.
So, let me cherish this priceless moment
For the present and for memory's content.

In deep darkness, yet this sparkling night,
A breathtaking, illuminating, compelling sight
Enchanting and echoing as I gaze sky-bound,
I experience a sensation of music without sound!

From 'Reflections'

ATUMN LEAVES

On a sunny Autumn's day
In the park, having a stroll
Watching children happily at play,
I looked up answering a silent call.

Saw few leaves from a tree falling
Dancing as dropping, smiling at me
Wavering, quavering, silently calling
Floating over a gentle breeze I see.

Mixed golden colours, sun kissed
Beckoning others to join in and play.
A touch to the senses, glad hadn't missed,
On floor many more leaves gather and lay.

Falling leaves' one last dance
In those conclusive final hours
Autumn's tapestry and trance
In tumult of pretty colours.

Bare boughs though wailing
Anticipating future's freezing frost
In Winter's naked dwelling
As the leaves finally are lost.

Revised 2024

AUTUMN

Summer sun slow-sliding down from high
And woodland trees beginning to sigh!
Verdure sun-kissed leaves gently fading,
Then, glorious Autumn colour's shading.

Colours painted by a Divine brush
Slowly losing Summer's green lush
In rustic red, bronze and golden yellow,
Shaken by chill wind's cruel blow.

Floating and falling in gentle breeze,
Descending slowly, dancing at ease,
Falling leaves leaving bare bough trees
Facing Winter's wrath, frost and freeze.

Wild life responding to nature's call,
Adapting to changes seasons install,
Migrating birds busy in preparation,
Others homing in on hibernation.

Autumn equinox negotiating the sun
For shorter appearance in daily burn,
Sun losing height, casting longer shadows,
Scarce few grazing cattle in misty meadows.

Seems not long when Spring was here,
Now howling wind ripping trees bare,
Few lonely leaves try longer to hang
From same boughs birds in Summer sang.

From 'Reflections'
2014

AZALEA

Between sunshine
   and April showers
Azaleas budding
   and counting hours
anticipating bud burst
   in an explosion
silently phased
   in slow motion - -
A dramatic fusion
   with aesthetic devotion
in impending rapture
   bursting in emotion.
Then,
   by marvel of earth's magical loom
buds transformed
   into miraculous bloom
scintillating
   and light enthused,
translucent
   and colour infused
like a spectrum of colours
   in a cascade,
like orchestral colours
   musically made.

From 'Flower Song'
Revised 2019

BABBLING BROOK

Babbling brook in intuitive motion
Free flowing in sedimentary erosion
Exploring and enthusiastic in emotion.

Rock and stones ripple forming
Together then aptly conforming
And in musical rhythms performing.

Birdsongs blending in total harmony
In nature's ornate orchestral symphony
All immersed in resonating polyphony.

In true sense of purity and wellbeing,
In peace and tranquility spellbinding
And in spiritual connotation transcending.

2024

BIRD IN A CAGE

A beautiful bird in a gilded cage
In a home placed center stage,
Struggle free life and bouncing
Away from predators pouncing.
But, the little bird wants to fly
Freely in wide open blue sky
Spreading her wing
Happily glide or swing.
Little bird's plea –
'Please set me free'

Set free out of compassion
Into wild survival from cushion;
Born and fed in routine devotion
Wild life an uncertain option.
Flying proving a clear handicap,
Domestic to wild life a big gap,
Parental protection long untied,
A misfit, companionship denied.
Fending off wild predators,
Food-fighting with competitors.

Grown lazy-wings in captivity,
Dreams of flying faded in reality,
Little bird failing to engage
Dreaming of life back in old cage,
Wild survival unable to endure

Soon back calling at the old door.
Little bird's plea –
'Please let me in,
Wider sky now I have seen
Living in the wild not keen.'

From 'This Mortal Chime'
Revised 2021

BIRDSONG

Incipient gleam of dawn embracing daybreak,
Dawn chorus celebrating sunrise as earth's awake,
Polyphony of mirth and merriment in the air
Heralding sound-sweetened Spring fair.

Plucking strings of Spring's lyre and lute
And songbird's melodic harp and flute;
Voices of Spring in sweet serenade
In an ensemble of pure lyrical cascade.

Hymns to the sun by perched passerine
On arched branches of woodland serene
In an oasis of calm and tranquillity,
In a wave of pure harmonic spirituality.

At day's end offering sacred evensong,
Carolling hymns to the Divine, voices strong,
In gratitude, thanks giving for the gift of life
And granting another day free from strife.

In inimitable ways nature's orchestra plays
And song birds' enchanting choral displays,
A lone voice or in chorus in total harmony
Adding floral colours to a choral symphony.

From 'This Mortal Chime'
Revised 2022

BLACKBIRD

Sing little blackbird sing,
What joy on earth you bring!
All Spring and Summer long
Perched happily you sing along.

Dawn chorus till evensong
Enchantment all day long,
In between you fly and flit
Searching for food to eat.

In contours of light and shade
Playing games of escapade,
Serenading in romantic phrase
And rhapsodies in nature's praise.

In my garden you add pleasure
You sing to me as I lie in leisure
Relaxing on Summer afternoons
I hear you sing many happy tunes.

Share with me, if you will, my pet,
Tell me your life's little secret;
Ever-cheerful, you play and chant,
Happiness you harvest, little you want.

Harmony with nature you capture
And in joy of living you enrapture.
Sing little blackbird sing
What joy on earth you bring!

Revised 2020
From 'This Mortal Chime'

BLOOMING

Hidden and intensely looming
Intent on that timely blooming,
Light and colour in tender fusion,
Colour composites in culmination
Out of sight in frenzied action
Bursting in emotional elation.
Then, buds in display sun-seeking
In final countdown silently ticking.

Obsequious in sun's warm embracing,
Unfolding as the Spring breeze caressing
And morning's pearly dews gently bathing,
Life incipient, expectant and breathing
And petals unfolding in slow motion
Finally, in bloom at height of emotion
Adorning and colour-craving for fulness.
And displaying in tumult of gladness.

2023

BLUEBELLS

In a hush woodland vale
Bluebells under Spring's spell,

Caressed by a gentle breeze
In lush blue hue dancing at ease.

Like the waves of deep blue sea
Under a green woodland canopy

Windswept, whispering in a spree,
Rays of Spring sunshine in glee,

In light and shade bound,
In laughter without sound,

Playing hide and seek
In a silent language they speak.

From 'Flower Song'

BUDDLEIA AND THE BUTTERFLY

Sky above is cloudless and blue,
Summer sun unfailing and true,
Buddleia in blossomed enchantment;
This must then be the prime moment
To entice that beautiful butterfly
With bright colour to catch her eye
And a sweet scent to further allure;
Then, at last, look who is at the door,
Butterfly on the threshold impressed,
Finally, close together they embraced.

2019

BUSY BEES

Busy bees on a mercy mission
Holding that benefactor's key
Humming in sweet nectar vision
Thriving in selfless generosity.

A playful potent pollinator
Between anthers and stigma
That prolific nectar hunter
Enchanting and an enigma.

In symbolic deep dedication,
Hard work and benevolence
And in creative connotation
Priceless devotion in silence.

Carefully collecting the nectar,
Absorbed in pollinating mist,
In duty a diligent benefactor
Performing in a prodigious tryst.

In that marvel of creation
Their enthusiasm and zest
From that act of pollination
Gathering the golden harvest.

Honey flowing from their fortress
That in intricate design excels,
Their hives of true happiness
In honeycomb of hexagonal cells.

2024

BUTTERCUPS

On a beautiful sunny day in May
Children out and about at play
Seeing first Buttercups of the year,
They look and then a loud cheer
As they see fields and verges glow
In multiple blooms of golden yellow.

Golden yellow dots in day light
Like twinkling stars in sky at night
These scintillating wild flowers
Beaming at their avowed hours.
Gleaming in May's festive rays
And singing softly in sun's praise.

(revised 2024)

CAMELLIA

When songbirds begin to sing
as a solemn tribute to Spring
Camellia's offerings
and endeavour
a vibrant visage
in vernal splendour
performing rituals
of Divine rite
appearing in red,
pink or white
blossoms in a silent repertoire
of musical moments in a floral choir.

From 'Flower Song'

CHERRY BLOSSOMS

In an inspiring interlude
                       in Spring
Cherry Blossom trees
                     adorning
in blooms
   of blushing pink flowers,
a ceremony
  Rite of Spring empowers.

With a sacred seal
            of sentiment
and boundless
      tide of merriment,
ecstatic
 in auspicious aura and felicity
in spectacle
    of exuberance and vivacity.

Measured in time
      by temporal presence,
treasured in memory
           till reappearance.

From 'Flower Song'
Revised 2019

CHILL WIND'S MONOTONE

Chill wind's monotone
And a melancholy undertone-
Wildlife hibernating,
Some birds migrating
And bird songs long faded,
Trees bare, wind raided.

Flowers once sun kissed
All hazy in memory's mist.
Frozen earth now in repose,
Dormant and nothing grows;
Snow and frost chilled,
But, hope and purpose filled.

West wind timely approaching
With expanding dewy wing
At chill wind's reproaching,
Birds eagerly waiting to sing,
Then, flowers will bloom again
And pleasure will replace pain.

From 'This Mortal Chime'

COLOURS

A golden glow
in the far east horizon
each morning,
I open my eyes
at sun rise
to a colourful life
unfolding.
Seven colours of spectrum
compressed in sun's radiant rays
feeding life
into all earthly colours
each proudly displays.

Imagine, at the origin,
when the earth woke up
in the early hours,
It was granted
a Divine brush stroke
of chosen colours;
sky screening the heaven
wished to be painted blue,
lakes, rivers, seas and oceans
desired to reflect parallel hue.

Plants in forests,
woodlands, meadows
and valleys all green.

Sun wore a golden crown,
moon a silvery sheen,
rainbow reflected
seven colours
that sun impregnated,
clouds wore white
then many shades of grey
precipitated.

Mountains merrily chose
scraggy grey
or volcanic ash brown,
some sheltering green vegetation
others in snow-capped crown;
birds, butterflies
and tropical fishes
allowed abundant dyes,
some animals camouflaged,
confusing predators' eyes.

King of the jungle
arrogantly displaying
golden brown mane,
In animal world
white, grey, black, brown,
striped or spotty stain.

Flowers, finally ordained
queen of all shades of colours,
adorned, robed and crowned
in life long glittering hours.

A blonde or a brunette,
eyes blue or brown,
rosy lips and cheeks,
colours glow and shine
when a woman
in her height of youth peaks.

With paints, palettes, canvas
and brushes of inspirations
natural vivid colours captivate
and capture artists' imaginations.

Human lifestyle creating
counterfeit colours dare;
ideas borrowed,
as nature quietly stare
at painters' palettes
and colouring brush stroke
and computer-generated
colours bespoke.

Colours in nature,
colours in boudoirs and bowers,
colours in gardens,
colours in wild flowers,

colours in attires,
colours in manners,
colours in cars,
colours in banners.

Colours bright and beautiful,
but not fed and fade at night,
starved and subdued
without the life-line
of luminous light.
With the lustre of light,
colours beautiful and bright
unfold
into a colourful world,
oh yes, 'tis a colourful world –
behold!

From 'Reflections'

CONKERS

Prolific, that Horse Chestnut tree
In Autumn's sweet sensation
Over-laden and breathing free
Those fruits in clusters hang on.

In prickly shells of lustrous green
Long they have waited silently,
Adorned ardently, picture-preen
On branches rocking them gently.

Sun-caressed slowly they ripen
Shaping, swelling from deep within
Then transformations happen
And time to burst through the skin.

Wind slowly gathers stronger force,
Then, conkers seen falling free
Lay on ground severed from source
Finally, untied from mother tree.

From 'This Mortal Chime'

COW-PARSLEY

Sunlight through the leafy woods,
                their faces beaming,
Countless umbels of Cow-Parsley,
                a beauty unassuming;
Such simple primal flowers singing
                silently as they sway
In this blissful woodland hideaway,
The sun-kissed umbellifers in
                un-inhibited gaiety
Reflecting a life short-lived,
                complete in jollity.

From 'Flower Song'

COWSLIPS

Light breeze and fair weather
Whispering merrily together
Watching Cowslips quietly gather
Covering the green meadow
With a hint of pastoral glow
And a tint of golden yellow –
Seen in visions of serendipity
In a meadow view of innocent gaiety.

Revised 2024

DAFFODIL

Daffodil, Daffodil,
I see you sway, then still,
In silent verse I hear you sing
Heralding advent of Spring.

Following Winter's repose
In early Spring you arose,
Windswept you dance
In a captivating trance.

As soft sunshine embrace
Your whispering grace,
Your golden yellow face
Glowing at height of happiness.

Haloed harbinger of Spring
What joy and delight you bring;
Spring fever on earth fuelling
In all living hearts dwelling.

Daffodil, Daffodil,
My heart with joy you fill,
Daffodil, Daffodil,
Stay a little longer if you will.

From 'Flower Song'

DAISY

Fair weather whispering Spring's in the air,
Warm breeze waving and Daisies appear,
Slowly unfolding their sleepy eyes
As the morning sun begins to rise.
In the fields and on the meadows
Under the sun and in the shadows
Countless blooms, in waiting many more
Pure white petals and a golden core.

Few impostors in painted petals, colourful,
Mingling, dancing together and playful.
Greeting walkers and joggers joyfully,
Then, pleading 'please tread carefully'.
Unbending and enduring plucking pains
As children, unaware, making Daisy chains;
And when the sun sets under the sky west
At day's end eyes closed for night's rest.

(revised 2019)

DANDELIONS

Peeping from their grassy nook
Take a look, take a good look!
A bright smile and beaming
A beauty in the wild unassuming.

Dandelions' bright yellow
In sunshine a promising glow,
Blooming with an inviting call,
Then, a gift of a unique seed-ball.

Those with unrewarding eye
Heedlessly passing them by
Disregarding the bashful beauty
Calling them weed what a pity!

A wild offering nature-intent
And vernal vivacity in adornment,
Sunlit faces sumptuously radiant
Praising the sun in wordless chant.

(revised 2024)

DARK CLOUD

Shrouding the sun
    gathering dark cloud,
Lightning corresponding
    and thunder singing loud,
Dark rain cloud responding
    to earth's call for moisture,
Rain feeding springs, lakes,
    rivers, plants and pasture.
 'Dark cloud'
    sun worshippers unloved adage
The heaven sent
    life-saving messenger in camouflage.

Apparent dark side,
    occasional lack of skill,
Overenthusiastic
    and a tendency to overfill,
Just as the mighty sun
    may at times overkill
Like the deserts of Sahara,
    barren, standing still.
Dark cloud breathing life
    in drops of rain,
Dark cloud holding the rein
    travelling not in vain.
Answering farmers' prayers
    with timely rain drops,

Rain clouds feeding the world
    with seasonal food crops.
As every dark cloud comes
    with a silver lining,
In dictum silver lining is
    earth's survival defining,
On arrival met an earth
    scorched and ailing,
Leaving behind
    sun shining again and earth smiling.

From 'Reflections'

DIVINE BRUSH-STROKES

Sun's setting after a day's work,
Night will negotiate in the dark
And promising another new day
Sun will rise again come what may.

Just before the sun's setting
Emotive clouds gently floating,
Colour-casting in playful imagination
Displaying magnitude of colouration.

Displaying a supernatural overtone
Of a natural phenomenon sky-bourn
Changing colours against the sky blue
Divine brush strokes of heavenly hue!

Besides the colour and the beauty
And unfailing sense of sun's duty
Deep in that ray of light shining
A potent power hidden, life defining.

From 'This Mortal Chime'

DOLPHINS

Breezy along the crystal realm,
A mirror of solitude and calm,
Hidden turbulence in ocean's deep,
Those wild hearts fearlessly leap.

Dolphins gliding over the wave
Free, frolicsome and brave,
Hearty songs and wild dance
On crest of the wave in a trance.

Enchanting and captivating,
Ever playful and scintillating,
Born free and fears unknown
In the deep or wind-blown.

Energized by that wild emotion
Contrasting leaps of graceful motion
Freedom's spirit in purest splendour
Simplistic yet a spectacle of grandeur.

On crest of the wave happy-gliding
In intense pleasure joy riding
Flying high then deep-diving
In freedom's opulent measure thriving!

2023

DURDLE DOOR

Down on Dorset's prehistoric Jurassic coast
A rock formed structure, an inviting host
Like a sleeping dinosaur, named Durdle Door,
Leaning from the cliff down to the sea shore.
Time tiered by rain, waves, snow and storms
Sculpted rocks and stones in unique forms.
Floating clouds flying by hugging the blue sky,
On crest of the wave rolling white waters fly
And when the sun's shinning and sky's blue
Reflections on water blue on blue imbue.

Scraggy hills and high cliffs proud they tower
Embellished by colourful native wild flower.
Autumn's floating fantasy by winged clouds,
Approaching Winter's hazy fog in misty shrouds,
Or, lightning sparkling with a loud thunder,
Then, snow-showers and frosty drapes under.
Changing watercolours and floating sky-scapes
Beauty beckons in all-weather landscapes;
Visiting crowd over-enthused, with trampling feet,
Nature, forgiving, with open arms ready to greet.

From 'This Mortal Chime'

ELEPHANT

Largest animal on land in the wild by far,
King's crown though humans didn't confer,
Yet, a graceful presence in appearance
With an air of pronounced regal radiance.

Not a killer, generally kind in nature
Rarely drawn to beastly adventure.
A social animal and family oriented,
Roaming in groups else ivory hunted.

Not a colourful animal to be seen,
In shades of grey wearing a thick skin,
Carrying a formidable weight
And moving in an unhurried gait.

A big beast and unique in feature,
Not beastly and calmly by nature,
Big head and a long-lasting memory;
Big ears, a trunk and tusks of ivory.

And ivory being a profitable commodity
Elephants fallen victims of human cruelty,
Falling numbers heading for extinction
At the mercy of poacher's will and action.

2024

ETERNALLY SEALED

In mind's spiritual light
Divinity still afar from sight.
Portent of shadowy appearance,
Or, some oracular inference,
Unfathomed those abstract signs
Given no finite defined lines.

Nature's beauty in purity's semblance
Reflecting Divinity's cryptic stance,
Measure and meaning well hidden;
Knowledge exploring, answers forbidden.
Believing in blind intuition,
Or, instinctive in imagination.

Creator's pronounced actions
Uncharted in human dictions,
Lifelong toil in devotion and duty
In contradictions and in ambiguity.
Purpose of life eternally sealed
And the mystery not to be revealed.

2024

FINGAL'S CAVE

Island of Staffa, a unique rock formation
In the Inner Hebrides standing un-eroded,
Birth-right from a strong volcanic eruption
In distant past, Fingal's Cave embedded.

Lonely in the middle of the open ocean
Clustered basaltic pillars cliff-forming
Confronting dancing waves' wild emotion
An uninhabited island cave wave-storming.

The exposed rock-gates of the hidden deep
A wild play-ground of the wind-driven wave,
Restless, hitting standing rock-faces so steep
Forming white-water crystalline by the cave.

Here composers configured musical themes
And artists' colourful brush-strokes re-living
Dancing waves emotional torrents extremes
And endless gush un-exhausted, deep diving.

Darksome whirling beneath the deep,
Fearsome giant roaring tides high-riding,
Lonesome rock facing waves' wild leap,
That rock exposed, fearless, not hiding.

From 'This Mortal Chime'

FLOWER SONG

Hives of happiness
           as flowers bloom,
Infectious smiles
           up-turning faces of gloom;
Flowers in fields,
           gardens and trees
Happily hosting
           butterflies and bees.
Veiled under haze
           or in morning mist,
Pearl dews shining,
           then dry as sun kissed,
Radiant and welcoming
           as warm sun glows,
Smiling and dancing
           as light wind blows.
Lightening heavy hearts
           feeling down,
An object of adoration
           and never a frown.
An object of beauty
           as beauty spellbound,
Melody as in music
           resonating without sound.

From 'Flower Song'

FORSYTHIA

Days are getting longer
Sun's shinning stronger
And as soft wind blows
West wind seems close.

Forsythia's bell-chimes ring
Intimating arrival of Spring;
Blooms of incandescent yellow
Reflecting in an inviting glow.

That colour-burst looming,
Countless flowers blooming
And radiant glow high and low
Moving with sun and shadow.

In hope for vivid regeneration
And coruscating in colouration
A meaningful message they bring
And silently then eagerly sing.

2024

FOUR SEASONS

Seasonal brushes painting
Many faces of nature,
Sketches of splashing colours
In framed picture.

Spring – nature's awakening hour,
Romantic hour, begins to flower,
Cattle grazing, sheep lambing – progenitive.
Summer – working hour, flowers to fruits,
Generating seeds, extending roots,
Snow caps melting, green, playful – productive.
Autumn – harvest time, filling the granaries,
Changing attires, moving sceneries,
Colours fading – ready for repose.
Winter – dormant, sleeping and slumbering hour,
In this blissful earthly bower,
Frozen, snow-capped – doors close.

An admixture in stages
Colours in contrasting light
In earth's seasonal passages
From sun's annual orbital flight.

From 'Reflections'
Revised 2023

FOXGLOVE

Born wild and free and stands
Well away from gardener's hands
Purple or white bell shaped flowers
Clustered in delectable towers,
Merry bells ringing soundless chimes
Foxglove singing in wordless rhymes.

FUCHSIA

As Summer sun
 rings a merry chime
Nature grants
 Fuchsia's dancing time
In shades of colours
 pure and delicate,
Bell-shaped petals
 immaculately ornate,
Dancing to finale of
 Summer tune till fall,
A fine performance
 deserving a curtain call.

From 'Flower Song'

GAZELLE

An eye-catching beauty in the wild
A captivating stance like a child,
A gazelle's cool and calmly presence
In that bare look of innocence

In wild habitat an allusive charm
And never meaning any harm.
Posture in poise and pulchritude
Then suddenly all void in vicissitude.

Once living in peace and tranquility
In contraposition of wild cruelty,
Now a sense of fear in disguise
Reflecting in those timid eyes.

Once gliding in grace, a happy face
Now stunned by a predator in chase
Running in fear and out of breath,
A fine balance between life and death.

Survival's sweet sensation in dismay
At fate's contemptuous powerplay
And in that ominous spell so cruel
Fighting fate, engaged in a duel.

Once nimble, graceful and gliding
Now life-stretching, speed striding,
Between life and death a very thin line
That in fate's conjuration set to define.

2024

HAWTHORN

Sun may hide and rain may bide,
Clouds floating, but sky looks bright
April on the way out and May in sight
Something brightening the countryside.

Walking in woods or copses or passing by,
Gleaming against the blue skyline
Soaking in the soft warm sunshine
Hawthorn's early blooms catching the eye.

In gentle breeze sounds of joyous whisper
From white florets of multi-bloom cluster
On leafy branches of lush green lustre
Resonating like music wafting in the air.

From 'Flower Song'

HONEYSUKLE

Wild adventure
        on hedges and hedgerows,
Or, on garden walls and fences
                happily grows,
Honeysuckle in shades
        of pink or light yellow
Quietly worshipping
        Summer's sun-glow
With an unassuming
        charm and grace
And with a beaming
        charitable face
Living in an invisible bubble
        of perfumed air
That everyone passing
        is welcomed to share.

From 'Flower Song'

IN A ROSE GARDEN

Entering a rose garden,
blissful is my mind,
welcomed by gracious smile
from each bloom,
a hypnotic power
able to lift all faces of gloom;
all my worldly burdens,
for now, left behind.

A vision of chromatic fusion
with changing light
in dramatic shades of
red, pink, white and yellow;
colours reflecting
warm welcoming glow;
in a rose garden,
beauty brimful in my sight!

Sultry roses sprightly,
happy and gay;
rose petals sun-kissed
under a blue sky
caressed by a gentle breeze
pearl dews dry,
playfully pursued
by sun's golden ray.

Crowned flower queen,
born to impress;
in a fusion of colours,
forms and fragrance
arousing dormant emotions
of romance;
a sensory bliss,
hint of nature's largesse.

Delicately designed petals
in silent rhyme
in lyrical expressions
of beauty sublime;
a beauty to behold
only in prime
before blemished
by temporal time.

From 'Flower Song'

JASMINE

In simple clusters of whiteness
Sun-kissed purity of brightness
And an ability to attract and allure
With a fragrance fabulously pure.

Admirers sweetly drawn unbidden
By Jasmine in a perfumed garden;
Fragrance-filled sensory adornment
In an evening of silent enchantment.

From 'Flower Song'

LABURNUM

Cold freeze at rest, a new day born
And vernal vivification duly sworn
As Laburnum's lavish racemes glow
In blossoms of incandescent yellow.

Radiant against a deep blue sky
Contrasting with an illuminating dye,
An inviting view of hope-inspired gaiety
In spectacles of regenerating spontaneity.

From 'Flower Song'

LAVENDER

A mixture of purple in blue
And blue in purple imbue
In Lavender's lush, lustrous hue.

Attracting bees and butterflies
And many more admiring eyes,
Under mid-summer blue skies.

On a happy note, a breezy dance
A distinctive flavour and fragrance
Conducive to fabled love and romance.

Avowed herbal remedy many favour,
An unmistakable and unique flavour
And culinary sumptuousness to savour.

From 'Flower Song'

LET THE GARDEN BE MY SHRINE

Let the garden be my shrine -
Sun's glowing or a spell of showering,
Songbirds serenading, plants flowering,
Here I sit contemplating the Divine.

The morning sunlight pure and purposeful
Wildlife's journey in simplicity stainless
And their freedom's birth-right painless,
Between light and shade clouds playful.

Verdant trees orchestrating all hours,
Glittering leaves bathing in dew
And aloft, the boughs' aspiring view,
Colours and forms in ornate flowers.

In a theme of endless cycle of creation
Advent of Spring and annual adornment;
Birth, beauty and joy of embellishment,
Then, decay and hope for regeneration.

Wildlife in sight and out of sight
Absorbed happily in their daily chores
Enjoying sunshine or defying downpours,
Then, birds, bees and butterflies in flight.

Sun, unfailing, fulfilling the daily round
And I realise dark clouds not in vain,

Clouds forming then storm and rain
Nourishing plants, soaking the ground.

Music in the air when songbirds around,
Scores of new blooms daily growing
Many others the wind gently blowing
And confetti petals decorating the ground,

Then, a starlit canopy of sky at night,
Or, cloud covered, obstructing sight;
When clear again watching in delight
Moons changing faces in soft light.

Spring and Summer's blossoming hour,
Autumn colours adorning the trees,
Frozen sculptures in Winter's freeze,
Expressions of earthly beauty in all four.

In perpetual seasonal cycles on earth
Colour choreography in creations
Within latitudes of thermal variations
Wonders of birth, decay and rebirth.

Tending a garden in season and time
Planting, grafting or sowing seeds
Watching them grow after many feeds,
Flowers bloom and sing in silent rhyme.

Wildlife playful in merriment and mirth,
Plant life radiant in colour and vivacity,
Awe-inspiring yet in apparent simplicity,
Gracious gift from bountiful mother earth.

Changing, changing, never is the same,
Light and shade playing hide and seek,
Colours and contours silently speak,
New plants growing wishing new name.

Splendour of earthly beauty in many forms,
What on this earth could be more pious
Than worshipping the most beauteous
That nature spontaneously transforms?

Let the garden be my shrine,
Colours in forms delicately designed
And purest beauty blissfully enshrined,
Here I sit contemplating the Divine.

From 'This mortal Chime'

LIGHT AND REFLECTIONS

Rays of light purposeful and enacting,
Reflections corresponding and co-acting
In opposite's perpetual prognosis
And in creation's cross-synthesis
In matters and in motions,
In energy and in emotions
Then, relative abstractions
From mirrored reflections.

Sunlight's silent emanation
Its potent imagery in creation,
At night shining on moons face
And reflecting in earth's embrace.
Then, light's emotional height
In seasonal variations delight
And in human minds levitating
In eclectic delectation scintillating.

Thunder and lightnings expressions
In rhythmic flow of wild imaginations,
Then, light's imitations in reflections
Glowing In mirrored orchestrations
Symphonic in musical connotations
And deep in emotional co-relations.
Divine choreography in action
Since the beginning of creation.

2024

LILY OF THE VALLEY

Don't know about the valley
I met her passing the alley
Not dark nor that bright
Sun throwing in enough light.

Lilly of the valley sleeping,
I looked at her peeping,
Then, I found her awake
And dared a double take.

An attractive innocent beaming
As if, smiling while sleeping,
Pure white blossoms blooming,
A simple beauty unassuming.

2024

LILY

Luscious Lily!
    An eye-rewarding sight
And her fabled fragrance
    set to delight;
A trumpet look-alike,
    close resemblance,
Melody in her core
    resonating in silence;
Delicately crafted
    in colours she wore
Symbols in colours
    embedded in folklore.

White for purity
    and depicting simplicity,
Shinning yellow
    bright as the sun-glow,
Pink promising prosperity
    and colour's verity
Orange glaring in stride
    In semblance of pride;
Journey between
    superstition and semantics
And images in realms
    of the romantics.

From 'Flower Song'
Revised 2024

LONE BENCH IN THE PARK

That lone bench awaits in the park
In daylight or at night in the dark,
Lonesome but inviting offering a seat
For contemplation or resting tired feet
Welcoming the visitors with a treat.

Rows of trees standing at the back
Negotiating sunlight and shadow's track.
A quiet seat for endless dreaming,
Or, swapping for dark mind's scheming,
On occasions, tired children screaming.

At sunrise a guiding spiritual sight
Under the mystic sway of holy light,
Sun clouds-free showing a happy face,
Spectrum of colours in cosmic embrace
And admiring beauty's luminary grace.

Trees between sun and the shadows,
Flowers flourishing in the meadows,
Reflecting leaves in sunlight coruscating
Then rustling in tune and orchestrating
And in human minds silently resonating.

Songbirds around and happy caroling,
White clouds on blue sky gently rolling,
People playing musical chairs unaware
Morning till evening when days are fair,
On a wet day no body's there, a lonely affair.

From sunrise to sunset offering a seat
Welcoming all visitors and ready to greet,
Free from commercial pecuniary obsession
The lone bench on a free for all mission,
Simple pleasure of giving in its vision.

At night's fall dark silhouettes haunting
And anticipating moments counting,
Daring phantoms in deep night's thrall,
Lone bench feeling shadow's soft crawl
And sun awaits the morning light's call.

2024

MAGNOLIA

Magnolias mute, but sing
A passionate prelude to Spring
With a whispering devotion
And flowering in profusion
In a sensational rapture
At this seasonal conjuncture.

Amongst vistas of vernal vivacity
Eyes set on magnolia's bare beauty;
As soft sunlight warmly embracing
And gentle breeze eagerly caressing,
Blossomed beauties in a trance
Swaying in tantalising dance.

From 'Flower Song'
Revised 2024

MARIGOLD

When Summer sun glows
When soft breeze blows
When welcoming blue sky
Inviting bees and butterfly.

Time now for marigold to unfold
Her blushing cheeks painted gold
Attracting her ardent admirers
As she buds, blossoms and flowers.

From 'Flower Song'

MEADOW FLOWERS

Far from casting shadows of city towers
Amongst those inviting meadow flowers
Singing silently as the warm sun caressing
And dancing with the cool breeze embracing
In pleasure spontaneous my heart's racing.

Under the canopy of deep blue sky they lie
Watching the white clouds go floating by
While lovingly hugging the green meadow
And playing with the sun and the shadow
Then, I joyfully join in without much ado.

And as I stooped down for a closer look
Their welcoming nodding heads shook,
Graceful beauty awaiting willing to meet
And with a smile warmly then they greet,
Unforgettable, O that spell-binding treat!

Inhaling whiffs of those mixed fragrance
Overcome by intense and inebriate trance
My craving heart in tumult of gladness
Away from city-life's confined loneliness
And daily grinds of consuming madness.

2024

MIGRATION

Ocean waves carrying sands
Depositing on faraway lands,
Sands flying from desert floors
Wind-blown to distant shores
And rivers run from mountain heads
All the way down to the sea beds.

Fish travelling miles in the ocean-
An objective theme of migration;
Migrating birds setting their eyes
Looking ahead in wider skies,
Animals searching for food
Leaving their roots for good.

And humans from prehistoric days,
Figured, for survival migration pays.
Migration's rough edge often brutal
Committed to survival at times fatal.
Fair or fiendish chance's future realm
Inviting with an illusive charm.

Up-rooting present's orientation,
Exploring a future in estimation,
Instigated by an opportune vision
Road ahead in an uncertain mission
Negotiating oblivion's ominous route
That never promised in degree absolute.

From 'This Mortal Chime'

MOONBEAM

Moonbeam my eyes follow,
Nocturne, in silence, I hear
And soft light in night's hollow
A serene sensation I endear.

Trees look stark and darkling
Shadows spreading deep cover,
Then stars in the sky sparkling
And moonbeam shines over.

Dark silhouettes keep haunting
Deep in that veiled night's thrall
And magical moments counting,
That in my sweet dream I recall.

In city light's bright electric flare
Moonbeam subdued in that glare
Emotionally muted in lost desire
In human evolution's eclectic gyre.

Clouds curious, floating they spy
Over vain phantoms in the dark
And walking shadows sees my eye
Then disappearing at dawn's spark.

2023

MOONLIGHT

Lonely moon stars in her sight
Granted no light in her own right,
Only borrowed sunlight reflecting
Earthbound and blissfully emanating
In silent motion that subdued light.

As sunlight tenderly embraces
Changing moon's nightly faces
New to full, then reverse phases
Soft light reflecting in stages
On sleeping earth's still images.

At midnight in moon's sight
A tender embracing every night
Between today's parting moment
And to-morrow's commencement
Witnessing the passing highlight.

Clouds at times creating shade
Moon smiles again as they fade,
Poetic emotion in silent melody
Of a romantic nocturnal rhapsody,
Or, a serene moonlight serenade.

From 'This Mortal Chime'

MOUNTAIN

Green the forest,
high the pyramid peaks in view
and the crowned summit
displaying changing hue,
heights ascending or
descending wave forming,
in rain and shine, fog and mist
or snow storming.

Snow-capped mountain
of rock and stone
or, in lush green vegetation
densely overgrown
or, forests of pines and spruces
in orderly rows
and in warmer clime
rain forest vigorously grows.

Hosting fearsome volcanic furnace
and craters
of lava of molten rocks
in massive incinerators,
some volcanic craters
alive and breathing fire,
some dormant and inactive,
lost burning desire.

Crater, plateau or pyramid-peak,
weather phased,
sunny, cloud covered,
snow-capped, misty or hazed;
some placid play grounds
in picturesque ski-slopes
or, challenging peaks
enticing brave climbers' hopes.

Climbing the highest mountain
conquering the peak
a challenge
adventurous men and women seek,
a challenge many sought
at their peril capitulating,
mighty mountain unphased
standing still, captivating.

Fascinated by springs, rapids,
riverheads or a waterfall
human and wildlife drawn
at mighty mountain's silent call;
rock faced, forest base or
volcanoes dormant or active,
caves, mines, forests, wildlife,
grazed or unproductive.

When mountains surround
and mingle with serene lakes
a transcending tranquil beauty
in solitude awakes
or, a lonely mountain

standing at ocean's edge
a magnitude of beauty sublime
at nature's pledge.
Great mountain ranges born
of nature's immense forces
hosting wildlife and hoarding
mineral resources,
creating and dictating
weather patterns, silently active,
captivating magical beauty,
seamlessly seductive.

Immensely productive,
evidently generous in giving,
on occasions, angry
and at times uncompromising
like a fallen face of an avalanche
of mounting snow
or, whirling molten lava
from a violent volcano.

Complementing overtones
of power and magnitude
while dwelling in a deep interfusion
of serene solitude,
mountains monumental presence
and the elements
performing balancing acts
interpreting ecological moments.

From 'This Mortal Chime'

MUSIC IN THE LANDSCAPE

Sunrise
with an optimistic overture
and a new dawn
like never before,
birdsongs
in dawn chorus enthral
with music in lyrics of
ardent mating call.

Rainbow sings silently
in seven colours
and symphony of ocean waves
all hours,
sea breeze transforming
in tranquil tunes
whispering,
whirling around sand dunes.

Rain in rhythms of dance music
or a rhapsody,
pure white snow, lyrical,
falling in hush melody,
sun and cloud singing
and playing hide and seek
over an enchanted forest
or a mountain peak.

Birdsongs in woodlands,
heathlands and vales,
high winds sing out
loud high notes in gales.
Visual imagery of silent serenade
in fog and mist.
Music in manyfold in felicity
or a melancholy twist.

Storm's venting tunes of
nature's fuming fury,
silence in tranquillity
or an interlude of flurry
like recitals of rippling
or rousing brooks
resonating as rambling
through wooded nooks.

Then dark clouds thundering
loud percussions
and lightning dazzling
in dramatic incantations.
Volcano's violent eruptions
and eventual escape
creating yet again
a new musical landscape.

Rills and rivers singing
a leisurely saraband,
wind ensemble resembling
a brass band.

Mountain echoing
as wildlife eagerly calls
and resonating sounds
of ravines and falls.

As birds singing holy hymns
in their evensong
sun's setting down
having sung all day long.
Then, the star-studded sky
singing silent night,
and moon's changing faces
serenading in soft light.

An audio-visual sensory
of creative motions,
emotive nature,
melody in her emanations.
Music in colour and contour
of standing landscapes
emulating equally
in changing sea and skyscapes.

Enjoying a beautiful landscape
in tranquillity
or, listening to
sacred musical offerings to a deity,
enchantment resonating
as wildlife rejoice,
euphony of sound
from nature's pure voice.

From 'This Mortal Chime'

NOCTURNE

Head resting on my soft pillow
Half through my dream I hear
Nocturnes I hear as I see moon glow,
Dreams I dream and sweet sensation
                              I endear!

Nocturnes I hear as I see moon glow,
Stars twinkling, sky cloud-free and clear,
Moonlight caressing silhouettes below,
Dreams I dream and sweet sensation
                              I endear!

Moonlight caressing silhouettes below,
Music I hear from the stars afar
Serenading from night's hollow,
Dreams I Dream and sweet sensation
                              I endear!

Serenading from night's hollow
As darkness knows no fear,
Restful and spellbound I follow,
Dreams I dream and sweet sensation
                              I endear!

From 'This Mortal Chime'

OCEAN WAVES

Living earth's heartbeat,
low and high tides in sequence
gently rolling crystal waves
in a mirror of calm
shore bound
in a harmonic musical cadence
and portals of solitude
in this serene aquatic realm.

Endless energy and motion
behind wave formations,
ocean waves emotionally driven,
wind ridden,
choreographed by wind's wild power
or soft emotions,
underneath the waves
another living world hidden.

A still world
of nameless, numberless silent graves,
relics of old civilizations
cruelly washed under water,
then, timeless regeneration
by the restless waves
and new lands and new lives
surfacing sooner or later.

Ocean's wealth humans sharing
and dangers duly daring,
awe inspiring, at times ruthless,
an overwhelming beauty
of immense power,
can be cruel and kills, yet caring,
an extreme edge of wild cruelty
complementing serenity.

The largest living creature
happily inhabit and die here
and the smallest invisible
without a microscopic eye;
sun, wind and the waves
busy charting out the weather,
without the elements
the living earth destined to die.

At sunrise golden rays curling
into wave's motion,
wind's gentle or wild emotions
shaping the course.
At sunset reflecting colours
competing with devotion,
and wind's unfathomed source
defining the force.

Tranquillity of watching the waves
breaking on shore,
source of life,
a haven for countless living organisms,
then in a changing mood

fighting ferocious tidal bore,
seeing through a mirror
of catastrophic cataclysms.
A living world beneath the beauty
of wave formation,
human over activities and over-tones
a cause for caution;
ever active, regenerative
and in constant reconfiguration,
ocean wave's unmeasured magnitude
in eternal motion.

From 'This mortal Chime'

ORCHID

Light in colours and colours in light
Beauty bidden by beholder's sight
With an impassioned appeal to delight

And when colour and light in fusion
In a process of chromatic elocution
Orchid appearing in a clear vision

Propagating with energy and vitality
Pursuing the path to height of beauty,
Intent and vying for lasting popularity.

From 'Flower Song'

PEBBLES

Under a clear blue sky
reflecting on a calm sea,
sitting on a pebble beach
my mind's free,
in my sight the waves
breaking at the shore,
picking a few pebbles
thoughts come to the fore.

Sea breeze and its changing
emotional expressions
reflecting on tide's force
and rhythmic formations,
then crushing waves in sequence
rushing to the shore,
washing down the silent pebbles
lying on the floor.

Pebbles are silent witness,
if only, they could speak,
would spell out many answers
we curiously seek;
colours not bright,
in soft mellow rustic shades
by restless tides timeless wrenching
colour fades.

Origin relates back
to earth's hard and rocky crust
shaped over time
by deep water's relentless thrust.
Each different and shaped
by ocean's power spell,
each survived long journey
and own story to tell.

Engrossed in my thoughts,
meanwhile, time moved on,
looking up saw the sun down
at the far western horizon
changing colours from yellow to orange,
then crimson red,
slowly disappearing giving an illusion
as if resting on sea bed.

Revised 2020

PEONY

Ambition for embellishment
                and intense activities
Amongst host of colours
                and floral creativities
Many discerning eyes set
                on a promised beauty
As Peony in her time
                unveils petals of purity.

Colour rich, in shades
                of red, pink or white,
Lively and bright
                caressed by soft sun light,
From bud to blossom
                exquisite in her prime
A blissful beauty
                abiding in transient time.

From 'Flower Song'

PERIWINKLE

On first day of Spring
Sun adding light hours,
Songbirds begin to sing,
Soon it's festival of flowers.

Pretty little periwinkle
With a deep blue hue
Expectations in twinkle
Arising up in clear view.

Riding on a green creeper
Feeding on sun and dew,
Shade of blue now deeper
Defining that colour true.

Spring-time waving so
In reply silently speaking,
Tweaking and rearing to go,
Dearly attention seeking.

2024

RAINBOW

Rainbow, rainbow in the sky
Radiant, colourful and clear,
Rainbow, rainbow soon will fly
And quietly then will disappear.

An arch of colours spreading
Against a shining wall of rain;
To portals of Elysium is it leading?
Or, is it mere illusion to entertain?

Sunshine reflecting on clouds of rain
Like melody in silence and in vision
Reflecting life of laughter over pain
That rainbow on a cheering mission.

Red, orange, yellow, green,
Blue, indigo and violet –
All in harmony, in heavenly sheen,
Seven colours divinely set.

An eye-catching archway sky-bound
A sight that enthuse and enthral
A profound beauty that astound
And heart-warming sight for all.

Rainbow, rainbow in the sky
Radiant, colourful and clear,
Rainbow, rainbow soon will fly
And quietly then will disappear.

From 'This Mortal Chime'

RAINDROPS

On that ocean wave riding high
Then aloft unseen flying in the sky,
A purposeful journey on track
Hidden raindrops on clouds-back.

Sun shining then clouds and raindrops
Bring smiles on faces of golden crops,
Coming again those seasonal showers
Refreshing the colour-face of all flowers.

Tree-tops busy drinking and storing
Enlivened by that downpouring,
Rills and rivers singing and dancing
Welcoming the rain-clouds advancing,

In Summer heat a shower cools
Creating puddles and still-pools
Then heavy downpours bustling
And gushing gutters happily yodeling.

When wind-driven and feeling strong
Dancing on roof-tops with a sing-song;
At night in bed restfully as we lie
Set to sleep by raindrops lullaby.

2023

RED POPPY

In repose, in her earthly bed,
Expectations raising her head
When the Summer sun above
Calling whispering of love;
Like flame of a candle fire,
Or, red lips of burning desire,
Red poppy's aspiration
Seeking avid admiration
And a popular appeal
With an adulating zeal
In a wave of luminous red enkindled
Countless blooms covering the field.

From 'Flower Song'

RHODODENDRON

Ringing merry bells
    in the month of May
In a delightful
    welcoming floral display!
A display of light
    and colours in fusion
In delicate shades
    of Rhododendron.

Radiance of colours
    in animated motion
And emotions calling
    for poetic devotion,
Festive fervour in
    few ecstatic hours
In exuberance
    and beauty of Mayflowers.

From 'Flower Song'

RIVER SONG

Rising from a mountain spring,
Intrepid, falling from a cliff-head
All the way dancing and singing,
Then, rolling on to a river-bed.

Running wild and paths free
Never feeling ever lone-some,
Verdant banks of trees in glee,
Humans and wildlife welcome.

Changing mood, threat of flood
Vulnerable banks overflowing,
Then again, spring flowers bud
On banks and gloriously glowing.

Restless river purpose filled,
Ripple song resonating all along
And the valleys whispering wild
The music to my heart's song.

After many turns and bends
Ocean bound at the estuary
A purposeful journey ends
The river living earth's artery.

From 'This Mortal Chime'

ROBIN REDBREAST

My little robin redbreast
In my garden in her nest,
Comes out when she sees me
From her nest in the tree.

Says 'hello, tweet, tweet, tweet',
Advancing close to my feet,
Not afraid, I am her friend
And like-wise she is mine to the end.

I offer her occasional treat,
She comes close, happy to eat.
Our Spring to Autumn routine,
In cold Winter we both stay in,
Don't see her much around,
Hear occasional flutter and sound.

At the advent of Spring
I hear her again tweet and sing,
With her mate in quest,
Busy mending her nest,
Raising her offspring to her best,
My little robin redbreast!

From 'Reflections'.

ROCKS

From mighty mountain heads
Down to the saline sea-beds,
From violent volcanic eruptions
To caves' concealed contraptions.

Iridescent impressionistic mosaic
That in nature's narratives strike
Creation's imaginative splendour
Pure, potent and unassuming ardour.

A revered beauty eyes may behold
And utilities promised many-fold
In gem's janitorial mother rocks
And quarries of building blocks.

From that base basaltic brown
To white snow-peaked crown
Imaginative structure and formation
Displaying creative core of colouration.

In caves' characteristic curvature
Nature's formidable architecture,
Blended beauty of hanging stalactites
Complementing standing stalagmites.

From peak, plateau and craters
To deep volcanic incinerators
That spell-binding splendour
And gripping structural grandeur.

Sandstones, limestones or basaltic
Between the tropics and the arctic
Rockfaces shinning in eclectic glare
And precious metals in hidden ore flare.

A factor in human civilization and culture
Reflecting in city-life's beauty and structure
Blended in its foundations and functions
And buildings architectural impressions.

Away from city life's frantic pulsation,
High against the sky a serene sensation,
That towering yet humbling rock-face
In peaked piety of solitude and grace.

Musical rhythms in changing hues,
Shadows' perspective and distant views,
Divinely devised nature's themes
Resonating in wildlife's sacred hymns.

Earth's original enduring rocky crust
From mountain peak to sand and dust
In many forms and formidable task
Wonders of creation in mystery's mask.

2024

ROSE

In true reflection of nature's ardour,
In a lavish seasonal floral splendour
Rose, assumed queen of all flowers
In a kaleidoscope of pretty colours
Appearing in pomp and glamour
In late spring till end of Summer.

Embellished in majestic attire
In grandeur of a silent fanfare,
Some spraying whiffs of fragrance,
Then, in gentle breeze a regal dance;
An authentic crown in realms of aesthetics
Reigning in the hearts of the romantics.

From 'Flower Song'

SACRED SHRINE

Deep in nature that sacred shrine,
Sun wind and rain orchestrating,
Birds caroling hymns to the Divine
And multi-religious codes consecrating.

Oracle may deliver a confusing speech,
Long echoes of meanings profound
Elements of nature eloquently teach
In reflecting colours and polyphony of sound.

In shades of light and darkness
Planet earth's ceaseless rotation
That stirred human consciousness
Of day and night with time's connotation.

That eternal search and quest
Staring at numbing spectacle of flaws
And that unquenching human zest
On a mortal scale defying nature's laws.

In shadows of high-rise bustling cities
Floating on a mind-bending ride
In a consumer carousel modernity's
Over-consuming generation of human tide.

Moral authority in quiet retreat
Admonished by a populist pulpit
Reconfiguring with rhythm of time,
Human progress in perplexed paradigm.

Hidden truth in riddles defining,
Values abstract but in wildlife shining.
Purity of life in sanctity of the Divine
In nature in holy spirit that sacred shrine.

2023

SHADOW'S VEIL

Sunshine and shadows coming in stages,
Scheming shadows casting dark images
And life's darkling shadows aroving
Pain inflicting and pleasure removing.

Tomb of dream in shadows subdued
In hushed silence deep in solitude.
Whatever grief shadows may give
Shadows move on sunlight will live.

Sunlight in pure goodness gleaming
Shadow's veil fiendish and scheming.
Between sunlight and shadows grey
Rocking on time's scale a trembling sway.

Love is that light that soothes the soul
Lacking that, swings in shadow's prowl.
Sun may throw light on danger's precipice
But, unable to reach shadow's dark abyss.

Those seekers in thrall of shadow's grasp
Fruits of existence escape from their clasp.
Without shadows a tendency to burn
Carried away by extremes, yet blissful the sun.

2024

SNOWDROPS

Nature blowing a silent clarion
Announcing Spring's on the horizon,
Sleeping Snowdrops in crystal rime
Just awake as Winter's calling time.

Then, shaking off the snowy dust
Rubbing down the frosty crust
In view sitting pretty and clear
Resonating in welcoming cheer.

Adorned in snow-white couture
Delectable petals delicate and pure
Snowdrops appear and silently sing
'Tis Spring, 'tis Spring, 'tis Spring!

From 'Flower song'

SNOWFLAKES

Miracle drops from the sky-
Snowflakes spurring the eye,
Brightness over dim darkness,
Or, sun shining over whiteness,
Descending slowly in silent melody
In serenade, nocturne or rhapsody.
Wind's ever-changing emotions
Setting the rhythms and motions;
Onward journey quietly beckons
And earthly beauty duly reckons.

Delicate and touch sensitive,
Intent and immensely creative
Figuration of fragile frozen filigree
Earth bound in a tantalising spree;
When the sun sets and moon wakes
Drifting, falling and gathering flakes
Layers over layers they all crowd
To a picture of a romantic shroud
Over frozen sculpted landscapes
Sparkling in multitude of shapes.

From 'This Mortal Chime'

SPIDER'S WEB

Reflecting radiant rays of sunlight
On a spider's web shining bright;
Spider at work eagerly weaving
A piece of art gossamer shined.

But, a shade of hidden cruelty behind
As a sly fly-catcher patiently waiting
With a dark motive intending to kill
A motive for survival, a stomach to fill.

From 'This Mortal Chime'

SPRING'S IN THE AIR

Sky's blue and weather's fair
Sensing Spring's in the air.
Leafy trees blowing sigh of relief
From bare boughs of Winter's grief.
Flowers begin to bud and bloom
Following Winter's chill and gloom.

Flowers first come into focus
Purple, yellow and white crocus
And delicate white snowdrops,
Then, the daffodil's yellow crops
Smiling in the mild sunshine
Beckoning the tulips next in line.

Primroses in pioneering spree
Adorned in purest simplicity,
Then a grand appearance on trees towering
The big blossoms of magnolia flowering
And like the waves of deep blue sea
Bluebells under woodland canopy.

Camelias in red white and pink,
Azalias await April showers and blink,
Full bloomed bounty in April and May
Challenging cherry blossom's glory day.
May's flower shows ablaze full blown
In colour choreography of rhododendron.

Migrating birds back in habitation,
Wildlife ending their Winter hibernation,
Robin redbreast busy building a nest
Others flying free enjoying Spring fest.
Woodpigeon, blackbird and tits in view
Appearance of butterflies and bees due.

Sun's Winter muffle is cast aside,
Floating clouds negotiating to hide,
Sun seeking to come out and play
Staying longer and warmer each day,
Sky's blue and weather's fair
Sensing Spring's in the air.

Revised 2024

SPRINGTIME

O that Spring sunlight
In a rejuvenating spree
A fountain of delight
In aspiration and glee!

Warm sun glowing
Sky above is azure
Light wind blowing
Lively trees verdure.

Blossoming of flowers
In tumult of gladness
And adorning all hours
Colour craving for fullness.

Ringing Jubilant chime
All in silent resonance
Singing praising Springtime
In eye catching presence.

Enthusiastically enraptured
In rhythm and rhyme
And aesthetically pictured,
O that festive Springtime!

From 'This Mortal Chime'

SQUIRREL

From sunrise to sunset the squirrel
Busy as if sallying in a hypnotic spell.
Work's their worship, fun and play
Hanging happily then swiftly sway
From branch to branch of a tree
In gardens and woods then running free
Displaying that fluffy tail in swift crawl
Then again climbing trees high and tall.

Chasing mates, cheerfully at play
On a clear and warm sunny day,
Then, a sight to behold and treasure
While eating, that devouring pleasure!
Digging holes, then hiding nut by nut
Anticipating freezing Winter's rut.
Life's purpose fulfilled by daily chores
And in same proximity play-time scores.

2024

STAR LIGHT

A canopy of stars never still
Eternity bound skies they fill.
Star studded sky countless in vision
A faint view of wonders of creation!

In the dark hollowness of night
Distant stars on nocturnal flight
On a long light years journey path
Twinkling, twinkling reaching the earth.

Numberless stars in boundless space
Many more eyes unable to trace,
Endless creation in ageless time
Stars in our eyes a beauty sublime.

Eternal light and force of gravity,
A creative phenomenon of relativity,
Super novas, red dwarfs and black hole,
Is there a Divine power in control?

Fallacies and fantasies had their turn
Romantic connotations may still run,
Now, science with a telescopic vision
And ever enthusiastic in that mission.

Generation science tirelessly spy
Testing advance telescopic eye
Looking deep into limitless sky
Human enthusiasm will never die.

Stars growing in distant galaxies,
Stars born in many human fantasies,
Starlight quietly fascinated human race
In silent melody and romantic embrace.

From 'This Mortal Chime'

SUMMER

Showers in April, flowers in May,
Come June, 'tis midsummer's day,
Summer sunshine, Summer breeze,
In Summer holidays life's at ease.

Parks, playing fields and village greens
Filled with echoes of laughter of children and teens,
Birds flying, resting or nesting on leafy green trees,
Blossomed flowers attracting butterflies and bees.

Families and children on holidays at leisure,
Playing on a beach an innocent pleasure,
Sea side promenades and on the golden sand,
Lovers take a stroll here hand in hand.

Farmers busy working in the field
Wishing a big and bumper yield,
Odd showers and the sun's golden ray
Help to grow the golden grain, so they pray.

Then comes harvest time expecting granaries full
Before sun dims, days trim and begin to cool;
Summer fun in Summer sun, a gift of nature
In earth's weather cycle a heart-warming feature.

From 'Reflections'

SUN SEA AND SAND

Sun reflecting on sea's azure hue,
Lull laying the smooth silent sea,
Absorbing and calming that view,
Away from daily chores mind free.

Sea's endless life generating spree
Eternity bound that holy mission,
In vitality holding that crucial key
And adapting in imaginative vision.

Sea like a mirror in translucent realm,
Sun glowing under a clear blue sky
Slow walking on golden sand, warm,
Sweet caroling as the sea-birds fly.

All my worldly worries left behind
Mind absorbed in nature's purest shrine,
Peaceful, restful and blissful my mind
Quietly contemplating the Divine.

2024

SUN SEASONS AND SENTIMENT

Spring equinox sets merry bells ringing,
Birds coming out and joyfully singing,
Plants foliage greener each coming day
Flowers intensely yearning for festive May.

In June, at the height of year's longest day
Soaking in high sun's warmth in its ray,
Then, time's over for June's brimming sun
Days will get shorter and it's Autumn's turn.

And as the Summer sunshine slowly fades,
Touches of gentle glow on Autumn shades,
Cool breeze caressing falling leaves gently
And the sun still trying to kiss them warmly.

Some birds will migrate seeking mild climate,
Rest getting ready for Winter and hibernate.
For the young, hopes of Spring rising high
But, for the old yet another year gone by!

Revised 2024

SUN WIND AND RAIN

Sun shining, wind blowing then rain,
Together they sing again and again;
Then weather forming – lightning sparks
Amid storm-cloud's thundering barks.

Storm-cloud's alarming advance warning
Wind and rain not for turning,
Array of lightning and thunder,
Then, field of muddy monochrome under.

Life in shadowy slumber in wet terrain,
Birds shaking in nests in wind and rain,
Leaves torn or holding on tirelessly sway,
Flowers ripped apart and blown away.

Then, wind navigating at high peaks,
Sea agitating and anxiously freaks,
Waves rising in mode multitude
Rushing to the shore mist imbued.

Sunshine helping living earth flourish,
Raindrops, in turn, soak and nourish,
Wind's emotional journey and touch-
In true measure none too little or too much.

2022

SWEET DREAMS

Lonesome that evening star,
Moonbeam soon shines over
Then twinkling stars from afar
Brightening the night's cover.

When the earth in night's grip
And the silvery moon beams
I am lying restful in my sleep
Immersed in my sweet dreams!

As the night sight sleep-wading
Through a monochrome vision,
In sun's absence colours fading
In depth of darkness and illusion.

Changing sky in deep night's thrall
Sleeping earth under dark canopy
Then, shooting star's rooted fall
And floating clouds look creepy.

Still immersed in my sweet dreaming
Under dark night's hollow cover
Starlit and the moon still beaming
Till the morning sun shines over.

2024

SWEET PRIMROSE

As Spring's early messenger
In modest pale colours you appear
Sweet Primrose!
On grassy banks you arose,
Or, peeping from woodland floor
And on rough turfs many more;
Sweet Primrose!
As Spring's hour grows
In warm sunshine or in shade
Your simple tufts happily braid;
Sweet Primrose!
Pure simplicity you dispose,
Modesty over exuberant vanity
As I behold your beauty in simplicity.

From 'Flower Song'

THE CLOUD

I am transient in the endless sky,
I am the mere mortals' celestial eye,
Without my probity they are destined to die!
Who am I?

I am the mother of a few that render
Storm, rain, snow, hail, lightning and thunder.
I work hand in hand with the mighty sun,
My work is never ending but, it's fun!

Sun draws moisture from the seas and the oceans
And impregnates me with feminine emotions,
In agony I roar and thunder before water breaks,
Once over in ecstasy I sparkle in a form lightning takes.

With rain I fill the lakes with as much water as it takes,
Fresh water from heaven after the sun bakes,
I add life to the mountain springs and rills
And the rivers running through town and country fills.

I bring back flowers smiling after being parched,
I nourished the earth that's no longer scorched,
I bring back the trees' colours bright and green,
Colours before my touch hadn't been seen.

Back above in the sky on my wing again I float
And as I do, I watch and spy and take note,
If the sun's too strong for some to bear,
For shades where needed I begin to steer.

In the evening's lull, if I feel playful and gay,
With the silvery moon hide and seek I play
Beneath the stars far and near twinkling,
Watching us play their eyes seem sparkling.

Once again, I float and I laugh loud in thunder
And I change attire many times, is that a wonder?
Amorous me, love to touch the mighty mountain peaks,
Then, sweetly steel a kiss or two on both my cheeks.

I see mortals bred, then fed and finally dead,
My celestial journey is eternal instead.
I am transient in the endless sky,
I am the mere mortals' life-line, do or die.

From 'Reflections'

THE SWAN

Memories of one late summer's evening
In a Berkshire riverside village of Sonning;
Enjoying a romantic setting, fine dining
By a window seat looking out admiring
The view over river Thames flood lit,
A bridge and a weeping willow in perfect fit.
In conversation and looking about
I mentioned that a swan missing out
To complete a picture-perfect view - -
To my amazement imagination came true!
A beautiful white swan appeared in view
And another followed to complete a pair too,
Appearing like a silent floating melody,
A pair of swans in a nocturnal rhapsody,
Floating freely and in deigned elegance
In silence, in serenity a pas des deux dance.

2017

TRANQUILLITY

Submerged in overcrowded pulsation
Of human motion and mechanical propulsion,
Gripped by a daily whirlwind trap,
Tranquillity is a rare gift to unwrap.

Seeking serene solitude somewhere,
And catching a breath of fresh air
Or, listening to many voices of nature
From mountain, ocean, woodland or pasture.

Admiring a crystalline mountain fall,
A spring, rapid or a ravine may enthral
And as exuberant wild life rejoices
Spiritual dimension in solemnity of voices.

Hushed woodland, in subdued sound, bustling
As birds singing and breezy leaves lazily rustling;
Many wild voices mingle in merriment
And pure earthly joy in echoing enchantment.

Ocean in solitude, waves in wind-swept leap
In relentless motion coming up from the deep.
Tide's changing patterns seem flawless,
Simple pleasures meaningful or meaningless.

Far away from those discordant noises
And distant that hollow hum of voices
City-life's bustling day there still echoing
And here in tranquillity nature's voices sing.

Life in haste, a blurred, blinkered visibility,
Clearer all-round vision in tranquillity,
An uncontaminated gift of Divine scheme
In solitude or in wildlife's sacred hymn.

Revised 2024

VOLCANO

Under a mountain-head a crater,
A deadly burning incinerator.
Loud eruptions, uncontrolled flight,
Dark ash-cloud screening sunlight.
Spewing magma of molten rock
And toxic gas causing havoc.

A natural phenomenon in action
Capable of complete annihilation
Falling freely from mountain height,
On its path dwellers in dreadful plight.
Away from striking distance a sight
And a simmering beauty may delight.

An energy in cataclysmic eruption
In a conducive act of destruction,
Changing the form and shape
To an entirely hostile landscape.
Years later a complete transformation,
Fertile land and new life regeneration.

Some hidden deep under ocean currents
In multitude of spewing volcanic torrents
And tsunami's existential devastation
Then in a twist new land formation,
Growing again plants and vegetation
And celebrating new lives in recreation.

Some are feeble, dormant or dead
Disinclined reaching the towering head,
Lost that flow of burning desire
In molten rock and deadly fire,
Fascinating few gleefully glow and entice
In that wonderland of fire and ice!

2024

WATER LILY

Gentle breeze
causing ripples in the pond,
Rays of sunshine
and occasional shower
Calling Water Lily
to bud blossom and flower,
Summer sunshine
whispering awaiting respond.

Well rested
from her slumber and repose
Answering to
many friendly and ardent calls
And a thought
of embellishment that enthrals;
Attired for the occasion,
in time, she arose.

Lily in full bloom,
her reflection in rippled water
Sun, shower and gentle breeze
in applause flatter!

From 'Flower Song'

WATERFALL

Rising from a modest spring
Trickles on trickles they sing,
Then, ripples on ripples gaining force
Away from emotional birth source
Rushing towards mountain cliff-head
In ecstatic sprint, rolling, surging ahead,
Dizzy height and rugged rock-face calling
Fearless and intrepid white-water falling
Care free and enthralled down-storming
Sparkling against rocks sculpture-forming
Reaching the lower ground creating a mist
Shining and sparkling when sun-kissed,
Then, behold! A beautiful rainbow looming,
A spectrum of colours hidden now blooming
In a spectacle of power and aspiring beauty,
Beauty and power shaping in uniformity
Together on a journey in total harmony
In poetic rhythm and unbound polyphony,
A purposeful mission, a tireless endeavour
Meeting a ravine, finally, destination river.

From 'This Mortal Chime'

WILD FLOWERS
BY THE WOODLAND WALKS

While on my woodland walk
I meet wild flowers, we talk,
We don't exchange names,
Yet, join in nameless games;
Lessons in pleasure of giving
And the joy of wantless living,
Contentment in simplicity,
Embellishment in vivacity,
Beauty in priceless smile
And as I leave after a while
I hear in soundless voice
Singing rejoice, rejoice.

From 'This Mortal Chime'

WILD FLOWERS

In Winter reposed frost chilled,
In Spring growing well healed,
In Summer plain pleasure filled.

Exposed in sun, storm and rain,
No disdain and never a complain
Enjoying fulness of pleasure and pain.

Smiling faces cheerful and radiant,
Playful, vigorous and jubilant,
Gladness filled in soundless chant,

Inviting many butterflies and bees,
Sun and the shadows equally please
And welcoming warm gentle breeze.

Short-lived, counting every hour,
Happiness hived, never look sour,
Every living moment they devour.

Positively purposeful and no repent
Even when old, withered and bent,
Wild flowers living to hearts content.

From 'Flower Song'
Revised 2024

WILD RHODODENDRON

On a beautiful warm sunny day
Enjoying floral festivities in May
Taking a stroll through the wood,
Suddenly, awe-stricken I stood,
A purple haze surrounding me
Wild Rhododendrons in glee,
As if, silent merry bells ringing
And countless flowers singing;
Enthralled, I looked around,
Enchanted, stood spellbound,
An experience this day I treasure
In core of memory, the pleasure!

From 'Flower Song'

WINTER

As Autumn waves Winter in
Days losing light at night's gain,
Sun's warmth day by day failing,
Gripped by freezing cold earth's ailing.

Looking at leafless, frozen trees,
Not in sight birds or the bees,
Farmers staring at frozen fields
Bare and barren, nothing yields.

Flowers of warm days fail to bloom
In frosty Winter's dreary gloom,
Snow showers and blizzards bite,
A panorama of colourless white.

Sculptured icicles and snowflakes,
Cold freezing wind and frozen lakes;
Frost bites then warming by fireside,
Homing in hibernation animals hide.

Some sporting crowds happily elope
To snow-capped mountains and ski-slope
In a joyous, playful, Winter wonderland
Like in Summer escape to sea and sand.

Santa Claus in his golden sledge,
For children, made a novel pledge,
Reindeers and jingle bells
Heart-warming fairy tales.

In winter sun's slow waning ember
Birdsong's fading, hard to remember,
Days of summer, warm and sun-kissed,
All seem hazy in memory's mist.

From 'Reflections'

WISTERIA

With a silent fanfare in Spring
   under a sunlit spotlight,
aspects of theatrical images
   on an imaginative height,
Wisteria hugging a wall
   or nestling in tiers
in clusters of
   sweet-scented flowers.

Tassel-like
   in sumptuous tint of blue
and some
   in white racemes in lieu;
Distinctive
   and decorative by design,
ornamental
   as oscillating in sunshine,
propensity of colour
   and light in fusion,
like a melody muted
   in vision.

From 'Flower Song'
Revised 2024

www.ingramcontent.com/pod-product-compliance
Lightning Source LLC
LaVergne TN
LVHW091322080426
835510LV00007B/613